WHIS OF PETTY CRIMES

WHISTLER
OF
PETTY
CRIMES

POEMS

EILEEN ɪᴋᴇ WEST

atmosphere press

Library of Congress Control Number: 2023902368

Published by Atmosphere Press (Austin, Texas)

Cover design by Beste Miray

atmospherepress.com

IN MEMORIAM

This collection is dedicated to
Stacey Shields, *Hunkpati-Brule*
And
George Floyd
And
Their Mothers.

And all mothers
On both sides of the veil,
Guiding children
Through
The process
Of dying,
Courageously
Showering
Light
Love
And comfort
Among
The Young
Who eternally need,
And
Wholly deserve,
Everlasting
Devotion.

TABLE OF CONTENTS

VAINGLORIOUS MOMCHILD

Call it what you will,
Give it any label,
Asperger's, autism,
Psychologically unavailable.
My mother,
Now lounging
In the Grand Upstairs,
Could've been the poster child
For a syndrome then unknown.
Like a bell that rings flat,
A holey sock affording no warmth,
The momchild in my growing up home,
Obliged everyone to shoulder the affliction
Alongside her.

Write best-sellers,
Splash movies on the screen,
Throw stories
Of outrageous success
Into the popular
Mind's eye.
And then
Thank whatever lord
Or lordess you believe in
That you were
Never related
To such a mother.

Over a lifetime,
Bitter brambles grow.
A rancid taste
Left in the mouth
The cheeks
On the tongue,
Gagging a child's life.

Entrenched walls thicken
'Til ceding a station
The youth can clamber atop,
Spread wings and fly.

MODERN HIS WAY

I.
A lilac-colored
Chrysler Imperial,
The Tesla of his time.
Purple for his "Jammy"
(Gramma to me),
One Chrysler
Cross country
Cross country
'Til worn down
To metal bones.

Then shows up
One brand new,
Same model
Color
A big, low boat
On wheels—
Whizzes by.
The road-ribbons
End in gravel
Dirt and dust.

Still keeps movin'
Cross Texas
New Mexico
Arizona Desert
More desert, 'til LA, CA
The coast
On one side, west
Then another, east
'Til road ends
In Atlantic water.

Modern for his time,
He boards
Prop planes
In Chicago
New York
D.C.
Criss-crossing
Criss-crossing
Criss-crossing
Ocean Atlantic.

Time and again,
Landing in Brussels
Boarding trains
For Antwerp
Walking
Walking blocks
Through the bejeweled
Chest of town,
In pursuit of
Diamonds raw.

Back in the US Midwest
Burrowed into one
Of his shops,
The crude becomes
Civilized—
Cut, mounted
Cast in wax molds
Unique settings
Rings by Gramps
Fit for midwestern queens.

All polished and bright
Under the tutelage of the man
Who grants me bristly
Moustache kisses.
Caresses
Hard and strong
So often shared with me
So special
His embrace
That of a ball player.

II.
Modern in his youth,
My Gramps pitches
Semi–pro baseball,
Minneapolis Millers league.
His club
The team of his
Four out of five brothers,
They sprinkle in and out-field
Adding vinegar and spice
To a winning lineup.

A crew of champions
Speckling a field where another
Diamond raw gets tamed,
Through the tossing
Arms and hands
Of a pitching man
Who modern in his dreams
Successfully wishes himself
Onto the score card
In local baseball's Hall of Fame.

While other men
Contemporaries
Want, desire, lust after
Cadillacs
(Another Tesla of the time)
Gramps' Chrysler Imperial
Would not
Could not
Be replaced
By another brand.

Playing ball,
He learns
Loyalty to the team
The Millers
The Chrysler
A certain make, model
And Jammie's hue.
Loyal to them all
'Til his old age
Grabs away the keys.

III.
Some call,
Consider,
Think the brothers
Stubborn
Bull-headed
Unforgiving
Un-forgetting
Holding grudges
To the light
Like diamonds.

To see the flash, the dash
The reflection
Of obstinance
Of hardest rock
Never to budge or break,
But scratch
Deep through glass,
Shattering relations
Battering bonds
Once thought forever tied.

But not always
Not even between brothers
That play together for years.
Even as men, a symbiotic team
Tossing serious ball.
This coin of brotherhood,
With loyalty on one side
Obstinance on the other
Constantly carried with a note
That states: "Trust in no one forever."

The note serves
As a long season's pass
To walk away, forsake all
Treachery unforgiven, not forgotten.
So far inside
The hard rock falls,
The heart's door slams
Betrayal remains alive
Takes on a life of its own.
One that lasts forever more.

In this clan, once renounced,
The pathway of trust
Might never be travelled again.
Instead, cross America
In your Chrysler,
(Or Tesla),
Beat a path
Fresh under the moonlight
New under the sun.
Leave beaten roads behind.

Stay away from those
Who cheat, lie, steal, stab,
Or otherwise, harm you.
It's the code of the family
In the blood
Now generations deep
Hard as diamonds
And not to be replaced,
No matter how modern
The man. Or woman.

HERE THEN GONE

I.
Post–WWII coupling,
Strangers,
Live with his parents
Work for his parents
Slowly get to know each other.
Try to be polite.
In due course
First child arrives.
Right afterwards
Another on the way.
Post-war housing available
Just in time.

Strangers no more
Polite no more,
They inhabit a penal complex
Of their own making.
Dating outfits off,
Battles commence.
They do not like each other.
There's no love between them.
Only lust.
His parents see it,
As problems erupt before
'The kids' move out on their own.

He wishes to leave.
Give up the job.
Miserable wife.
And hellish home.
Give voice
To his wanderlust,

Find work offering
FREEDOM
From the oppression
Stooping his shoulders.
So slender and young.
He wants to drive truck.

"No! No! NO!"
Shouts shrewish wife
Again and again.

His mom whispers,
"Sorry son,
Dad needs you
In the shop."

It means being
Home with *her.*
Her, her, her.
Plus two
Then three
Kids, kids, kids.
And of course,
Duty, duty, duty.
Here (home)
There (work)
And everywhere.
No escape for him.

Until the war at home
Escalates to extreme.
I'm a small child
Awakened from slumber deep,
Overhearing shouts, shrieks, threats.
"Not happy?"

He screams the obvious.
"I'll gladly leave for good,
Give you *that* divorce."
Something a five-year-old
Six-year-old
Seven, eight, and nine-year-old girl
Never wants to hear,
Loving daddy so.

II.
Sadly, the battles rage on.
The alarm sounds often.
Finally, he turns into
That independent trucker,
Coming home to Minneapolis
Between cross-country runs,
Working for companies he likes,
Taking jobs that pay him well,
On teams that treat him right.
His dream of travelling,
Of freedom in his grasp.
He's happy on the road.

Of course, the loveless marriage shatters,
Finishing the destruction
Started long ago,
It continues over months
Years.
A little girl,
I'm stuck at home,
With mom in misery.
A mom dispensing demands
Like a despot:
Do this…do that…do it again.

My work, labors of love
Not good enough
Never good enough.
Still, *doing this…and that…*
Over and over,
Until Dad's splendid silhouette
Dims the doorway
And he sweeps my little body to his own.
In a flood of relief
I grin without end.

Whatever divorce is,
He hasn't done it to me.

Hours charge by,
The war between adults
Dampened by absence,
Eventually flairs back ablaze.
His affection for the kids
Somehow challenges
Mom the manager's reign at home.
The girl is confused, torn,
Tries not to cry.
Loves dad for his defense;
Fears mom
For any punishment to come.

Competitive to the bone
The dismal woman, the fuming wife,
The vengeful mother,
Ensures this pattern
Sets the nature of relating
For the rest of time.
A child loving him most,
I try to prove
My love for Mom as well.
Take the abuse
Attempt to improve
Be perfect.

Seeking faultlessness
In all mom has me do…
And do…and do again.
A little one who never gives up the race.
Until one day
Deep into adulthood,

Like Dad,
She speeds off—
Singes the door
And burns all bridges
Between them
In her haste to escape.

III.
Thus, wanderlust passes on.
The need to get out from under the mat,
Avoid being stepped on and squelched,
Dodge that life of duty and drudgery,
Passes from Dad to me, the girl, her siblings,
Maybe even generations to come.
The combatant fires that pressure-cook childhoods,
That parents flame with bellows
Of growing animosity for each other,
Can leave the young with one indelible impression:
In movement, there's joy.
Travel, yes,
See the world, yes.

Let the spirit flow
Teether it not.
Be the rushing river
Not the solid rock
Nor even the lake
Of water standing still,
Collecting algae
And decay.
Do not listen
When others advise,
"Moving can wait—
Stay still."

For some to go, to prowl,
Is not a decision.
It's a soul-deep drive
Not to be ignored.
Not for long.
The itch to roam sets in
Often and hard.

The dam on lake's end breaks,
Rocking the boat, sending it out and away,
'Til Dad, child
And others,
Once here, are gone.

AKIN TO ANEMIC COWS

Back in the mid-twentieth century,
Before the ink dries on my birth certificate,
Declaring my given name Eileen,
I'm dubbed with the nickname "Ikey"—
And a shortened rendition sticks
Lifelong.
Begging my pardon, people ask:
"How'd you come by Ike?"
Often as not, I belt out the entire saga,
No glamour here—quite the contrary.
My mom gets pregnant two months after delivering her first.
Baby #2 (me!) pushes out one month earlier than due.

Mom's parents race off their North Dakota farm
To reach the Twin Cities,
Excited about this tiny hatchling
In the warm incubating box.
Standing side by side outside the glass,
They study me
Their lil' weakling,
Weighing less than three pounds.
Lying like a corpse, limbs stick straight,
All skin, bones and blood veins.
A long silence ensues.
Then Grandpa announces:
"Now here's a human Ikey, if I ever saw one."

In the barn at home,
He's left, emaciated from hoof to horn,
An anemic cow named "Ikey".
Grandma elbows him in the ribs,
Crafting an emphatic declaration of her own:
"Don't say that! She's beautiful!"

I hear this story plenty
During childhood.
Mom never fails to assure me,
Beautiful, I was not. Not at all.
She laughs, I never do—
Not at all.

Grandpa's favorite occupation?
Teasing Grandma.
Frustrating her no end,
He calls me Ikey
Forever and always.
Like a fire ablaze,
The shorter Ike catches on
Among family and friends.
At school, I'm strapped
With the formal, Eileen.
Never fit me.
Not at all.

Years later, at my first teaching job,
I share an office (and phone) with another Eileen.
People worry confusion might rule our days.
But the two of us laugh at the quirk of fate.
Like me, she never answers to the official.
She's permanently referred to as Sam.
Immediately, we take a short-hand path to friendship.
We're two women discarding the obvious for short, manly,
Three letter nicknames: Sam and Ike, Ike and Sam.
By then, it's undeniable, Ike is who I am.
But, I no longer resemble an anemic cow.
Not at all.

PASSING SECOND GRADE

School days
Unreal
Surreal
Little there
For the likes of me.
Going through the motions,
The drills
Math, English
Science—
Whatever the subject
I'm a ne'er-do-well,
Not doing well at all.

A lost soul
With an awkward body
A withdrawn mind
Going through motions.
No wonder:
At night I doze, not sleep.
Then, morning,
I'm shackled,
A second grader
Who can't yet read or write
chained to books.

Principal Phil-in-the-Blank
Holds parent meetings in excess,
Discusses my scholar-osis.
His counsel: hold her back.
Repeat the same grade.
Dad balks
And at home
Under the glare of sewing lamp small,
Perched next to me on a piano bench long,

He drills me
In the printing of one word: Eileen.
My first name.

Every night
For weeks
I repeat
Repeat
Repeat
Write on the page,
"E-i-l-e…"
And stop there.
I'm nervous.
Palms sweat,
His body
So close.

His eyes
And voice
So tender,
Keeps me
On the bench.
In my body,
I try to let
Shyness slide
Feelings fade
Except those kindled
By his being there,
Next to me.

One evening, mid-quest,
In a spate of despair,
Dad mumbles, "It's crazy!
You make one 'e'
But refuse to write the next."
He's right.
Torment shares the bench with us.

Yet Dad's view surprises me.
There, on the piano bench, under the lamp,
I know confusion largely blooms
Over my first grasp of earnest,
Fully-present parenting.

A puzzling cypher to scratch.
I had no label
No reference
For tenderness
Devotion
Feeling inordinate safety.
It's not alphabet letters
I refuse to finish.
Instead
I prolong
The closeness to Dad.
I savor it.

I end each day, Dad beside me
A treat to sample slowly
The last lick of flavor postponed.
Eventually at his behest, I learn
To write, read and spell.
One thing does not change:
In school, I'm average at best.
Shame with such gifted siblings.
Brother #1, the brainy,
Brother #2, the sporty.
And in between I'm the sister,
Barely passing second grade.

STOPPED SHORT

I.
My brief soft-ball career
Begins and ends in Junior High.
There, I sparkle until a line drive
Does me harm.
I get no attention.
Don't want it.
An injury so evident,
The taped, bulbous hand
Cocooned in rounds of Ace.
The pain, the pounding—
I can hide
In my room, door closed.

Now brothers
Share my chores,
And grab greedily
At the attention
I shun.
Young Brother #2
Weeds the garden
Next to the drive.
Unable to make out
A blade of grass from a rose,
He grumbles, "It's *her* job,
Not mine!"

A token number of thistles
And dandelions
(The largest in the plot)
Are plucked
And lazily piled
Beside his feet.
But then, pal Pat
Tromps over from next door.

Gardening left for the birds,
Cowboying more their style,
The two whoop away
Off down the drive.

Flapping arms,
Holding invisible reins
Off invisible bits
In the mouths of horses,
Only they see—
Except maybe the refracted eyes
Of the bumble bee
That follows the boys
Down the lane,
Perhaps those eyes see all too well.
Flap, flap, flap goes young Brother #2,
Sting, buzz, sting goes bee.

Under the arm
Deep in the pit
In the flap, flap,
Flapping to follow,
The stinger's hammered
Into Brother #2's skin.
Hits tender target
Slams the bull's eye
The duct, then the sweat gland,
Brimming with poison plenty.
Flap, flap, flapping no more,
Screams take center stage.

Brother #2
Little grade schooler
No gardener at all,
Makes a bee line
To the house,
Car, doctor,

And comes home
With metal apparatus,
A contraption
Bigger
Grander
Than mine.

Poor cowpoke
Gotta hang up his spurs
Keep arm in the air,
Up, up, up, off his body.
Brace strapped around his ribs
Neck, shoulder
Hot, itchy, miserable.
Infection sets up house.
Doesn't budge.
Won't leave his underarm.
Then leaves and comes back.
A recurring nightmare.

No more flap, flap, flapping,
No more invisible reins
On imperceptible horses.
No more horsing around,
Not for Brother #2.
Not that summer.
The silver lining:
No more weeding either.
No more gardening, at all.
Sister chores gone,
Like others heretofore
Pronounced in his name.

II.
Up next,
Eldest Brother #1.
Now all chores
Fall in his lap—
Mine, Brother #2's,
And any already assigned
By management aka Mom.
A high school honor's student,
The task he hates most,
Coming 'round most often,
Asking the most of him:
DOING DISHES.

Washing and drying.
Putting away
Breakfast, lunch and dinner.
A despicable imposition.
But Brother One, the family genius,
Scientist, and inventor,
He's ready to turn
Dish Doing
Into Scholarship.
Hours now spent measuring, analyzing,
Then doing it again—all for the sake of
Exploring new home economic vistas.

Hours spent
Determining
Correct amounts of soap,
The exact depth
Of bubbles,
The precise fill of water
In the basin,
That might allow foamy suds—
Not the liquid—

To cascade over sink's edge,
Then, across the rubber mat
And onto the floor beyond.

More mathematical projections
Needed to propel
Dry dishware into cupboards.
Expanding dish doing efficiency,
He stands, legs spread eagle,
A specific distance from the counter,
Where cups, bowls, and plates
Line up like little soldiers.
And then, on some internal cue,
Brother #1 lobs individual
Plastic Melmac specimens
Toward the wall of shelves.

Times, nine out of ten,
The dishes miss their mark,
Go astray and boomerang back
In his direction,
As if the cabinet spits at him.
Brother #1's dish doing acts,
A sight to behold,
At least for a while,
For Brother Two and me.
Mom never appreciates
The impromptu performances.
Although there's a chance to catch one
Three times a day—before his kitchen run abruptly ends.

That's when Brother #1 takes on
A tall, wide urn.
A rebellious jug
Cast of thick aluminum,
Stored on highest shelf
Near the ceiling.

Launching the heavy missile
Again and again,
Failing to reach the heights,
Again and again.
The young scientist, inventor, scholar,
Grows angry, tired, reckless.

Finally, one rebound
Downright does him in.
The metal beast
Clean and bright
Bounces off the wooden shelf
And comes back to bash
Him in the eye.
"OOOOOOW-CH!"
That vicious vase deposits the seeds
Of a mean, black shiner.
Tender and sore,
It swells and darkens instantly.

Had Brother #1 been an athlete
Baseball pitcher
Or hockey goalie
Like Brother #2,
His fumbles may have
Stayed on aim.
But lobbing away, fast and wild,
Another abhorrent object
Flies at him and clatters to the floor.
But not before Brother #1 jams
Three right-handed fingers
Blam!
Into the cupboard door.

"YOOOOOOW-CH!"
Howls Brother #1
Oldest son
Eye ablaze
Finger broken
And in a cast.
He mustn't
Do the chores
Not now
Not his
Not mine
Not any.

III.
That summer of mishap
I can honestly say,
My injury,
My taped hand
Comes from catching
A line drive
In soft-ball.
Brother #2 has to admit
His trussed-up body
Stems from riding
An imaginary horse.
So embarrassed is he.

Then there's big
Brother #1
High school honor's student,
Could not, would not
Admit his wounds
His black eye
His braced and bandaged hand
Result from doing dishes.
So, the genius sibling
The inventor extraordinaire
Creates a new story
On the spot.
The first time someone asks,
"How'd you get a black eye?"
Then notices his hand,
"What happened to you?"
Without skipping a beat,
Brother #1 quips,
"Got kicked by
A Canary—"
(A theatric pause)

"Broke my finger
Wrestling it
To the ground."

I wish my injuries came
Adorned with a snappy retort,
But not in the cards.
Still, his excuses cheer me.
Inspired,
I jump from the bed
And resume my chores.
I do dishes and weed gardens
With one hand, slowly,
But I'm never as slothful
As Brother #1, the Dish-Doing-Wonder,
Or Brother #2, who abandons work for play.

For a short time that summer
I am part of a well-oiled,
Well-run girls soft-ball team.
But my career in the women's league ends
Before it can bloom.
Just as well.
Most of the time
I play dutiful middle child
And pick up the slack
Of my completely lame
Un-oiled, poorly run, family team,
(The last word used damn loosely).

SUGAR AND SHADOW

I.
It's Christmas—and I'm eight years old.
5 am, dauntingly dark,
Those plum fairies
Still dancing,
And we're in our cave
Of a bedroom.
Knotty pine walls,
Our cocoon
Walls hated by mom,
Who never wants *HER* home
To appear cheap and tacky.
What others might deign a mere cabin.

Walls loved by us,
Three kids to a number,
Living in a two-bedroom
1950's bungalow.
Surrounded by woods,
That rub elbows with a swamp.
The cabin-esque spread
Gives off frontier airs.
Renders us
Kid pioneers—
Daniel Boone, Davie Crockett
And Annie Oakley reborn.

"Hey! Hey!
Wake up—"
Young brother,
Brother #2 whispers
With the urgency of a shout:
"Hear that?"
Mhm-m-m...mhm-m-m...mhm-m-m...mhm-m-m...

Nighttime fog clearing from my head,
My ears,
I *DO* hear it.
Non-stop.
Mhm-m-m…mhm-m-m…mhm-m-m…mhm-m-m…

There's distress acute and plain.
Wide awake, Brother #2 and I
Listen hard.
"It's a baby,"
I offer a hunch,
Alarmed by the prospect:
A baby appearing
Like magic
On a crisp Christmas morn.

Mhm-m-m…mhm-m-m…mhm-m-m…mhm-m-m…
Without pause
The whining goes on.
"From the living room!"
Brother #2 speaks loudly now,
The side of his head plastered to the wall,
As if to gain x-ray vision
Through his ear.
After all, knotty pine's the only thing
Between him
And the tormented bawls
On the other side.

Circling his body around like a crab,
Brother #2 skitters off the bed.
Solemnly, shoulders squared, back straight
He marches off, out to explore,
Investigate the fright—
Daniel Boone reborn.
Within moments, the crying stops.

Two, then three, minutes pass,
And the youngest, I now imagine being eaten
By the crier, no longer a baby
But a hungry ogre who's fooled us
With childlike yelps.

Slowly I inch away from my warm blankets,
Slink to the doorway and peek 'round the corner.
Heart thrumming in my chest,
I spy Brother #2 on the living room floor,
Huddled next to a huge cardboard box.
I tiptoe up next to him, lean over the side
And there in Brother Two's hands,
Wriggles a baby alright.
A puppy black, white tip on her tail.
Issuing a Merry Christmas squeal of my own,
I lift her from the box—best present ever!
The white-tipped tail leads to the name, Sugar.

II.
We grow up, frontier kids
With a sidekick,
That fun, fluffy-eared Sugar.
A Full-breed Spaniel
With official papers,
It never keeps her from being a true pal,
Hunting treasure and exploring wilds.
One hot August day
Years after the first winter,
She wanders alone and free
In the field out back,
Only to bring home her own pet.

An all-black puppy, mostly Lab,
Sprightly trots along behind her.
Sugar tolerates the spry juvenile—just barely.
But not so for the Lab,
Who likes to interfere
In Sugar's affairs.
For the pup,
Dog bowls set and rise,
According to the ventures of Sugar.

We learn something new
From Mom, Home Manager,
She calls Sugar's pet
"That loose mutt!"
Or "Stupid stray!"
(There's no formal "feral"
In the common vernacular, not yet.)
But we kids give
The new dog in our midst
A proper name.
She's dubbed Shadow.
Full name: Sugar's Shadow.

Hating "that loose mutt"
Mom never calls
Her *our* name,
Never calls her at all.
As much as she hates
Knotty pine in her home,
She hates letting
"That worthless thing"
In the house.
The dog stops at the door sill,
Threatened by a swinging broom
Off the long arm of Manager Mom.

Shadow, who tags along after Sugar
Everywhere—
Could not, did not
Trail her into the house.
Even in the dead of Minnesota winter,
When everything freezes,
Shadow, "that vile stray"
Curls in a shivering ball
On the unheated back porch,
While Sugar inside,
Enjoys warmth within the walls
Of "cheap and tacky" knotty pine.

At eight and nine years old,
I spend hours in bed
Awaiting sleep,
Contemplating the day past.
Mulling over my world's affairs.
I stare at the knots in the pine,
Seeing the lack of certain design,
Working out in their chaotic patterns
Eye balls, noses and mouths,
Faces full,

And I wonder:
How does a person hate?

How can people hate wood or walls?
Hate a dog that comes loose
From somewhere else,
Then comes home,
Comes to be here, to be ours
In a loose sort of way?
Answers elude my reach,
So eventually I settle my mind,
By making hope-filled vows
That I never hate.
Certainly, not so much.
Not like *that*.

Shadow,
As much as she adores
And wants to be like Sugar,
She is not and cannot be.
She stays through one winter,
And then like she came,
The Lab is simply gone.
Maybe Mom browbeat Dad
Into carrying away "the stupid mutt"
Taking her a far, far distance,
Never to return.
I suppose it's so.

After Shadow's disappearance,
Sugar and I share
The porch stairs each evening.
I imagine our suppers,
Sugar's in a bowl,
Mine on a plate,
And picture the loose dog
Scurrying back to us.

But then it grows dark enough
For me to admit
Shadow is gone. Truly gone.
Worse: departed she will stay.

III.
Years later, I trek off to college.
Sugar remains at home.
I'm back at Christmas break,
Breathing in the familiar smells
Of cookies in the oven.
Soothed by traditional
Decorations on the mantle,
Wrapped presents under the tree.
All is well.
"Where's Sugar?" I ask.
Mom, matter-of-factly replies,
"Well, dead, of course."

Then, she turns and walks away.
Away from my shattered world,
And ruined holiday.
I bolt after her—
"What?!" I spit the word at her back.
"What do you mean?"
She stops and cocks her head in my direction,
"I'm sure I wrote you."
A statement sounding so flatly factual,
I could almost believe her.
"The dog got sick.
We put her down."

She never wrote,
I never knew.
That holiday season,
I go back to school early.
In college I learn and see lots of things.
Many outside the classroom,
And often for the first time.
I see "loose women of the streets"
A label spoken with the same adult prejudice

My mother demonstrated years earlier,
Hating "that stray, loose mutt" Shadow.

My junior year,
For the first time,
I bus to rundown neighborhoods,
Dilapidated tenements,
And work with "disadvantaged" children.
An intern, I am exposed to
People judged and shunned
With the same hatred
My mom first demonstrates,
When maligning life
With knotty pine walls.

I learn while at university,
Parental prejudices
Come in various shapes
And sizes.
Some in the shape
Of dark circles in blonde wood,
Others in the size of a loose black Lab,
Tagging along behind a smaller
But alas, pedigreed Spaniel.

What I truly grasp is how insidious
And how easily overlooked
Is the grown-up discrimination
That passes to children,
One generation to the next.
Flashed at the young,
Packaged as
Sugar
Bigotry commonly
Too frequently
Dawns in the realm of
Shadow.

WHISTLER OF PETTY CRIMES

I.

I say goodbye
To Gramma's famous friend,
The summer in between.
Between high school and college.
Goodbye Minnesota.
Hello Arizona.
The summer in between.
That sizzling hot, mostly lazy,
Laid, more than back, laid down
Specifics, the law
And torment—
Cap that Southwest summer of '67.

Specifics laid down in Sedona,
Two rows of travel trailers,
Laid out in tight lines
As if awaiting the end of a zipper
To plow through and bring them close,
As if expecting someone,
Something outside
To pull occupants from the A/C inside.
It would be, must be early morning,
When the heat simmers low,
Before noon when summer's pots
Turn to full boil.

Before noon when steam from the stove
Of slender sidewalk
Of bleached gravel
Between the unzipped RV teeth
Might evaporate freckles from delicate skin,
Like those on my slender teen-age legs.

The morn, early, it'd be,
Who sounds the alarm,
Drawing people outdoors,
Emptying one tiny trailer after another?
Gramma's notorious friend,
With her legendary voice.

Every morning she practices
(Every day of every year),
Under an awning,
Aside a tooth of the zipper composed of RV's,
And punched into the wooden porch beneath,
A music stand, holding pages
And pages of notes
Sent by post to Sedona Arizona,
Special delivery or hasty courier.
Musical and other notes—
Sheets of notes, with margin notes,
(It's '67, long before Post-Its).

There—
Now, hear it?
The siren sounds,
Tweet, chirp,
Peep, cheep,
Tweet,
Warble and hoot.
Each sound
Scripted in the notes,
The special delivery,
Laid into specifics,
The law to be followed,
Set down for Hollywood.

Gramma's friend and neighbor,
A bird imitator,
Renowned for creating
Every sound,
And song,
Tweeted, warbled
And trumpeted by a feathered creature,
In every movie
Cartoon
Fantasy kingdom
Ride and concession.
She tweets, warbles, and hoots entire fantasy worlds.
Every morning
Without fail,
She rehearses.
Broadcasts the signals
To eager ears,
Like Gramma's, mine
And those of many
Friendly neighbors.
She zips us quickly together,
Packing the air
With every chirrup and coo
Imaginable.

II.
Among the others
I stand silent, eyes shut,
Giving myself over
Going to the birds.
There—
Now, hear it?
Pa-chip-chip-chip
Peep, peep,
Cheet-cheet,
Warble-warble-whoop.
Each sound
Scripted in the notes.

Eyes closed,
I do not see
The Whistler's
Dark side,
Not composed
Of sweet bird song,
But the screech
Of jealous vulture
Ambitious Owl
Or another
Power-hungry
Bird of prey.

In a park of loosely zipped
Oldsters,
I'm fresh meat.
The Whistler,
Begrudges my Gramma,
Who keeps me to herself,
Except for the hours she naps,
And I swim laps in a pool

Too often shared with
Another predator of sorts—
Giant cockroaches,
The size of rats.

I'm all Gramma's,
Except for the early morning hours
I spend off-roading
In the Red Rock Country,
Sacred to the Hopi Elder
Gramma hires to guide me,
Exploring sights from his open jeep,
Hearing stories and prayers for the land,
Withheld from the zipper people,
But shared openly with a girl keeping eyes closed,
And listening to the song of bird, wind, rock.
They are not hidden from me.

One such absent morning,
After the Whistler imitates bird voices,
She corners Gramma with a plot,
Hatched in her wily mind.
A ploy to get attention
Back where it belongs.
Not on Grandmother and Granddaughter,
But back on her,
The zipper people's Bird Whistler.
Her line to Gramma goes like this:
"The girl can make college cash,
Work each day for me."

Never wishing to disappoint Gramma,
I clean the Whistler's small house, porch, and patio,
I stoop over laundry, wash, and iron,
Clean some more—often
In the same spots as earlier.

Cook and bake,
A burning coal,
I toil day in, day out, hours at a time.
Hate grows for every chore, and the shrieking Whistler.
Gnashing her teeth, she finds fault with everything.
Dishes—still dirty, knick-knacks—still dusty,
Fresh bed sheets—put on topside-down.
In my 18 years, no one tells me
Bed linens, (only plain, flat and white at the time)
Have specific upsides, laid down as law by some Etiquetteure.
I quit.
Retreat back to the small, welcoming haven
Of the most pleasant person in my world.
Gracious Gramma, the only soul who assures me,
I am a cherished, treasured child.
Like always, she opens her door, her arms, her heart,
And accepts my pronouncement of 'job-over'
Without rancor, disapproval, or one bad word.
Not a peep.

III.
The summer swells hotter by far.
Still, each morning, I'm drawn outdoors like the others,
Eyes closed, ears perked, awaiting bird songs,
A flock of uplifting calls
From the throat, the lungs of the first
Duplicitous person I rub up against.
There'd be more over time,
But like first love, this one stands out.
Perhaps the chasm between the soft whistling
And the rasping screeches of a woman
Driven to cruelty by inner birds of prey.
Simply grew too much for an innocent girl.

Then again, maybe it's forever fused
In my mind with the tragedy to come.
Awhile after gaining freedom from the Whistler,
I'm about to share lunch with Gramma.
Helplessly, I watch as her back stiffens,
And convulsions pitch her from chair to floor.
My mind races—did she take a bite?! Is she choking?!
I do not know.
Standing in a rigor of my own,
I stare with horror at what my eyes cannot believe,
Her body spasms, jerks, violates the apathetic air,
Minutes pass, moments drag—time I cannot tell.

I run, run, run away—out the door
Across the sun-bleached ground,
Arrive at the house I know best, cleaned too many times.
Racing onto the porch, surprised to hear someone scream:
"Help! Help!"
No bird song now, only grief,
It's me, disillusioned by events passing fast,
Out of control—police called, ambulance summoned,
Phone calls, phone calls, phone calls on lines, numbers
Distinct for every service, numbers I do not know.

Someone cries out, sobs—out of control.
It's me—I wail over things
I do not know.
Help arrives, not soon enough for me,
But for Gramma?
I do not know.
I'm shuffled into the back of a patrol car.
Scanner-radio blares. Fan blows warm.
Above the rear window, sun beats hard.
Burns my skin through the glass,
My neck, my shoulders,
Burning thoughts:
"I did things wrong, *wrong*?!"
"This is my fault—*mine*?!"
"Please, please, let her be okay! *Please*—"

IV.
I sit in the car ruthless eternities,
Parched shoulders slump.
Weeping, praying, wishing—
Then, I don't know how,
But I'm no longer there,
In the back seat, alone,
Lonely in Sedona, in Arizona at all.
I leave, check out,
Mind wafts through the rear window,
Like the sun, I glare at the me on the seat inside,
Deserving what I get,
Having done Gramma wrong.

I figure things out.
I'd seen Perry Mason episodes plastered across TV.
I'm off to jail for what I did badly.
Feeding Gramma food to choke on,
Staring at her contortions,
Not using the phone, not knowing the numbers to call,
(There is no 911 in every city, everywhere).
I couldn't even remember the number at home in Minnesota.
Feet frozen to the floor
I couldn't move, until I ran away, ran and ran.
So late, I leapt for help,
It too, part of my crime.

The phone number at home, Gramma would know,
She's too far from me,
Might as well be on the moon,
That far—
Instead she thrashes on her kitchen floor,
Gathering attention from the zipper-tooth people,
As if the Bird Whistler practices now.

I know better, this is no whistling,
There are no songs,
Only bursts of anguish coming from the cop car,
The choking throat, the panicked lungs,
Sounds surging from the girl's—my own—breaking heart.

A policeman comes back to the car, Bird Whistler in tow,
I look for her then, my Gramma. She won't exit her nest.
Every other instant the ambulance lights
Flare and die, flare and die,
Giving me hope they'll fix her,
That she'll revive, get back in her chair.
We'll have a late lunch, happily chat, "Crisis averted. Whew!"
Yet, at the back of my mind, now back in the car,
I realize I'd been sent to stay with her
That hot, sizzling summer,
Because she's sick, (always been sick),
And this time—maybe sick enough to die.

I guess I knew it could happen. But did I, really?
No one told me, the details kept secret,
A story unfit for a young lady.
This too, part of my crime,
I am young, too young to care for anyone,
Steps away from death.
The policeman pretty much says so,
As he indicates I must go with him now.
Burdened with guilt and regret, I do not argue.
Through the side window, I signal good bye
To the Bird Whistler, gone so very sour.
I'm driven away. Without seeing Gramma.

Not getting to say farewell,
It's what I deserve for my crimes.
Off to jail. Court. Then prison.

But we pass the jail,
Where I expect to be thrown in a cell,
We pass the courthouse,
Where I expect to be sentenced,
Instead, the cop stops on the edge of town,
Outside the bus station.
He buys me a ticket home to Minneapolis.
I weep from one end of the country to the other,
From Arizona to Minnesota,
I shake and shiver in the freezing A/C.
Have no sweater, belongings, purse,
Money for food or drink.
It's what I deserve for my crimes,
Especially the biggest of all—
Letting Gramma down.
Would she forgive me?
Ever let me back in her door?
I do not know.
Perhaps not. I'm too inexperienced
To help her stay well.
I do not know. I am not told,
If my parents are aware of my arrival,
If they'd pick me up at the bus terminal.
I am not told. I do not know.

V.
My mom meets me, my dad long gone.
Driving like a madman, 'cross country,
Off to Sedona, Arizona,
Where he'd say goodbye to *his* mom, my Gramma,
And gather my stuff—things I never got to do.
Not that it matters.
Mom tells me in her gravest voice,
"You know, she died."
I do not know, but see gramma there,
One of the zipper-tooth people,
Zipped into the undertaker's bag,
There on the floor, as our lunch looks on,
From the table above.

It doesn't matter—
Not anymore,
If our sandwiches go stale.
It doesn't matter
That the bird whistling turned sour.
I am too young,
My Gramma dies in my care.
It's criminal.
In my youth,
I am sure,
Absolutely,
Without doubt,
The crimes are mine.

There is no funeral for me to attend.
I'm home in Minnesota, curled up on my bed.
Uninvited? I do not know. It does not matter.
It is what I think I deserve.
Mom dishes out Gramma's things
To family, friends and her zipper-tooth neighbors,
I receive nothing—feeling it as punishment
For what I failed to do,

When unknowingly charged with keeping Gramma alive.
A sour taste in my mouth,
For years, I suffer the memories,
Too many birdsongs, too much pain.
Time passes, the hurt subsides, and confusion clears.
I finally understand:
I was *told* to care for Gramma,
I was *told* to clean the Bird Whistler's home,
I wasn't *prepared* to do either.
Nor was I readied to face
The death of the person I loved most.
Then, I was eighteen years old,
My gramma fifty-four years young.
Now, I finally understand:
That scorching hot summer in Sedona,
The crimes were many—some grand, others petty,
But none were mine.

CLUED-IN CANADIANS

It's late…
Late '60's,
Late night.
We're talkin' trash.
Late night trash.
Trashin' the man,
Trashin' war,
Trashin' all those
Trashin' others,
Who trash draft dodgers, hippies,
And still others,
Trashin' the pristine environment.

It's Duluth,
Northern Minnesota.
Spittin' distance (almost)
To Canada.
Canadian kids
Share the dorm,
Sit on the floor,
Spittin' distance (literally)
From us city kids.
Twin Cities' kids.
Canadian kids listen politely,
As we city kids trash.

It's late…
Late 1960's,
When border lines
Are strings to jump,
Not walls to scale.
So, we sit
With Canadian kids,
In equal number.

It's late…
Late at night,
We're all
Young and innocent.

Despite Viet Nam,
Water- and other gates,
We're young and naïve.
And we city kids trash,
Protest our pants to threads.
The Canadian kids,
Bystanders,
Fascinated with us,
Yes.
Yet more so with differences
Between our government,
And their own.

On the US side
Of the border string,
Our's spews fear by saturating markets,
Media campaigns
Anxiety weeds
Proliferate,
Choke out the bloom
Of carefree youth.
"Don't Litter"
"Recycle"
"Clean Up This Mess"
The onus is on YOU!

The world's a-stew,
A heap, a tangle,
Polluted,
Destroyed—
And YOU did it,
With your litter.

The critical message,
The star-spangled belief:
Every person in the nation
Individuals all,
Are responsible for what ails
The whole.

Kids of Canada,
Young and innocent,
Hail from a country
Wanting kids kept that way,
Innocent, unburdened,
Thus, their campaign across the media:
"Relax, kids of Canada. Yes.
Corporations, manufacturers, factories,
Pollute. Wreak havoc.
Not to worry. We'll take care
Of big picture problems
Created by them and others."

The critical message,
The plainspoken belief—
Problems of a nation
Need solving further up the chain.
Corrections are not
The responsibility
Of singular persons.
For Canadian Kids,
So clued-in to differences,
Their government *cares*,
While on the US side of the string,
Government *scares*.

In the late 1960's,
Late at night,
Sitting in the college dorm,
I learn lots from
Clued-in Canadian kids.
But none more essential,
More freeing,
Then my gaining a litmus test
To measure government crusades
And their media marketing claims.
Things I use off and on
For the rest of my days.

FATHER IN THE CAR

I.

My father died years ago, from cancer.
I'm sure he welcomed the relief from constant pain.
Always a funny man, a clown, an ace at lighthearted mischief,
My father tossed levity into the mix of everyday.
He settled his family on Lake Minnetonka,
Where he grew up, third generation.
He knew in winter deep, where the lake froze top to bottom.
During bitter cold, on days off from work,
He drove around, kids piled in the back seat.
With the road hugging the shoreline,
Dad picked his spot and hollered,
"Hey, kids! We turn right or left?"

Rapid fire, we called out the shoreline direction,
And to our utter delight, he guided the car off the road,
Out across the surface of the lake.
He turned the wheel in one direction, and then another,
The auto-turned-sled slipping
And sliding in circles on the ice.
After letting us whoop and yowl, giggle and snort,
He'd steer back onto the road,
And things settled to quiet,
Until dad warned:
"Don't ever, *ever,* do that,
Without your father in the car!"

Years later, I learned to drive.
Dad took me out in the car alone—to concentrate.
Nervous and excited, I showed off new skills,
Still, there came a dangerous mistake.
Dad stayed calm, didn't chide or criticize.
My recklessness passed,
The car back under control,
No damage done.

Spawning a relieved sigh,
Dad's lone comment:
"You don't ever want to do *that*
With your father in the car."

II.
Every summer we wound our way
Through Dad's favorite parkland,
The Black Hills of South Dakota.
Progressing slowly along spaghetti thin roads,
And twisted switch backs, mile after mile,
Dad paid attention to curves.
Our job in the back seat: watch for bears.
Oh, how important, spotting dark brown grizzlies.
At every sighting, Dad stopped short.
We studied the creatures, as they approached the car.
The best days get marked by sightings galore,
Bears coming to gaze back at us through the windshield.

Sometimes, if lucky
And dad sensed little danger,
He rolled down his window just far enough
To offer a banana to a bear.
That way we saw up close the animal eating.
When the final bits of fruit got yanked from Dad's hand,
He slowly closed the window,
Put the car in neutral and rolled away.
Once at a distance, he drove off
All of us silently contemplating what we'd seen.
Soon Dad broke the moment's magic
Spouting his legendary line:
"Don't ever, *ever* do that,
Without your father in the car."

Each trip through the Hills
Dad stopped at Mount Rushmore,
Not only to see faces carved in the rock,
But to check the visitors' center
For the *Lakota* Holy Man
Ben Black Elk.
The very best Black Hills days?

When we fed bears
And discovered Black Elk
Fulfilling his vision as ambassador
Between his native people
And those of the world beyond.

Holding great respect for the elder,
My Dad stood across the room,
Rounded us into a huddle
And gave a pep talk,
Like we're getting psyched to play ball.
Show respect for this Great Man! Dad coached.
Assume the proper greet-Ben-Black-Elk mind frame.
Then, one at a time, he released us from the cluster,
Watched us walk solo across the room,
And extend one tiny hand in friendship,
Thanking the Grandfather and his people
For sharing their lands. With us.

Just six, or eight, or ten years old,
Bubbling with trepidation,
I dragged my way across the floor,
Practicing what I'm to say.
Once in front of the Holy Man,
I nervously stared at his feet and mumbled words
Like those Dad suggested.
Taking my small sweaty hand in his giant paw,
Grandfather Black Elk smiled broadly,
Shifting the hundreds
Or thousands of wrinkles
On the most ancient face I'd ever seen.

Perhaps it's these times
As a small girl growing up,
My dad instilled in me
Love for South Dakota,

And regard for the Tribal People
Who keep the Hills Sacred.
Now when I drive through the area,
Nothing feels quite the same.
No bears roam free,
And the aged peacemaker passed on.

Times change, but my affection for the Hills
And the Tribe remains strong.
Dad, I thank you for that.
Too for all the playful moments in childhood.
It's the air of hilarity about you,
I miss most.
Of course, still today
I recall your advice.
Please know, dearest father,
Whatever roads I take in life,
They'll never, *ever* be the same
Without you in the car.

2020: A YEAR OUT OF HAND

A lost cause, the world of transport
Can't be counted on.
Not now, not at all.
Not at all what I expected
When packing,
Leaving home.
Not at all what I expected
Waking up halfway 'round the world.

Despite best intentions
Nothing moves:
Roads blocked
Borders blocked
Minds blocked
Tickets issued, refunded, issued again.
Planes abandoned; airports deserted.
Passengers, what about them?

Accepted, rejected,
Glazed with fear
About what'll never come.
Crumbling, tumbling
Ideas of safety
Melt like ice
At the poles of world non-sense,
Global no chance.

No chance to move,
Go forward with plans,
Circle together with others.
Friends, old or new,
Partners, or colleagues,

The aged, or young.
Cancel? Cancel!
No-go? No-go!

Everything's a no-go,
Unless courting quarantines,
A two-week reserve
Proves no bother
Or inconvenience.
No problem this:
Isolation, desolation, divestiture.
And fear over what might never come.

Ideas of safety
Slipping, sliding
In the minds of power
From the mouths of men who decide
The fate of all.
Stay apart,
A constellation of
Far-flung detachment.

Many tiptoe forward
Looking back.
Hoping, praying, wanting
What once now seems like long ago.
The old 'real' so very attractive.
Looking back
To eateries, malls, school, work,
To all that went before.

A future merely mirroring the past?
What charge of comfort, happiness,
Does that promise?

Why not do more, do better, go beyond?
At least grab the chance to stretch
Past what's been shattered.
Move to higher ground,
Seek an altruistic pathway.

The world might embrace
Feminine, nurturing
Ways and means.
Not as radical rhetoric
Nor fantastical musings,
But rather the collective cry of women
Itching to mend the cultural shards
Painstakingly sidestepped by men in power.

Yesterday's men,
Yesterday's power;
Both should be history.
If only.
If only the world's people
Weren't hiding in fear.
If only the race
Had not gone adrift.

The political race,
The race to consume,
Pillage, rape, amass, and colonize.
The race to win the whole board.
The human race aimlessly adrift,
While glazed in fear
About what might never come:
A facsimile of the past.

Now at center, a germ.
No stench of mustard necessary
In this gas.
Not this time.
The masses suck in fumes,
As plumes waft by,
Pixel, after sickening pixel,
Ration, after galling ration.

The 'viral' blips:
Believe this germ is,
Must be, cannot be anything but,
Our modern mustard.
Spread at your own peril.
Until peril, and the threat thereof,
Is the germ,
The kernel of belief that blooms.

Not alone. There's another impulse from center line,
Again, given pixel by unquestionable pixel:
Be sure to thoroughly "STAY HOME!"
And slam every door, in every face—
Even when it's the appearance
Of those you love.
On the flip side: go out at your own peril,
Or the illusory threat thereof.

The next bunch of boastful, beastly blips
Are spawned at the center
Not only to inform, but sooth,
Any restless, rebellious individuated inklings.
"We deliver!" in bold neon letters
Prepared, unprepared food,
Medications—whatever you need,
All bait for the trap "…at home…"

Suddenly governments around the globe,
Those destitute (supposedly) institutions,
Pinpoint bins, brief cases, drawers of funds
Secreted away,
And never tapped,
Not for the destitute urban or rural poor,
Reservation tribes, or survivors of natural disasters.
No government had enough to help all of them.

But now, today, we are to trust,
Men at the center line
Creating our beliefs, our reality,
Out of the blue,
Unearthed magic money piled
Deep in the bowels of government coffers,
Enough to dust off and save the world.
SURPRISE! Suddenly billions to fling about.

Go ahead, pay Joe Schmo down the street,
And Cory Corporate Head fallen in the red;
But realize,
Until this latest world-shattering crisis,
Governments anywhere, everywhere,
At the center informing beliefs and reality
Sang a different tune,
Meant to placate, but never soothe.

The boppin' fairy tale went like this:
"We have debt, mounds and mounds of debt."
Token bail outs for you,
That's the best we can do,
All we may grant!

It's true—if only you'd buy the refrain:
"We have debt,
Mounds and mounds of debt."

Having heard this before, (again and again),
Curious minds now query:
Who pays for worldwide salvation,
In the case of global home delivery?
How do governments afford economy-sized relief,
For each and every family,
Within each and every country?
Who exactly is due gratitude in bulk?

The bail out by multi-nationals
Stands stalwart at the center,
Informing all,
Including governments world-wide.
Big Corp, content we sleep, wake and
Glue eyes to pixel after pixel,
Swallow "home delivery" while jailed inside,
With beliefs about peril in mind, right on top.

'Parent' companies,
Rich as can be,
Now inform humanity.
The message:
"It's us at center line,
Spawning greedy tenets on top,
Peddling life for the masses
At bottom rung."

Once the church would've
Offered salvation,
But then,
Governments stepped in,
Relieving this
And granting that.
Both church and state
Took turns at center stage.

Now, today,
A fresh lineage:
No cardinal or pope,
No queen or king,
President or Prime Minister,
Instead, a CEO,
PEO, OEO,
And every other EO imaginable.

During the cross over at center line,
They don't cut checks,
Just evacuate funds from illicit accounts
To dump into civic treasury chests,
Politician's brief cases, or somewhere
Deep in the bowels of government coffers,
Now dusted off in order to revive the world.
Hocus-Pocus! There're billions to fling about.

And the grateful citizens of every country,
Called by leadership at center line:
"Consumers"—Ta-da!
No citizenries anymore, anywhere.

Now inhabitants of
Reality-on-the-bottom are
Regulars who use up, and use more.
Abracadabra! Consumers.

In the freshening at central hub,
One belief hangs tight:
We are consumers,
Grateful for home delivery,
Awaiting the end of perils (or threats thereof),
And showing thanks, kowtowing, scraping bottom,
In deference to EO's mid-wire,
meddling with, and revising all.

Beliefs marketed and media-lized,
Corporate heads dictating what to think,
When and how, pixel after claptrap pixel,
Burying life at the lowest extreme.
Voilà! Real life at the bottom of things.
"It's the only way,"
Cory Corp'rat swears,
"To compete, to race."

Indeed, we're to believe
The competitive race
Offers bargain-basement rates,
Savings at rock bottom,
Deals with lifetime guarantees,
All passing us safe and sound
Through a prowling cloud
Of global germs.

However,
The harm foisted on us,
Infecting the world,
Is not so easily erased.
The fix is not available at bargains,
Or rock bottoms,
Guarantees, lifetime or otherwise,
Notwithstanding.

The fix is not
Isolation,
Hand soap or disinfectant;
The problem is BIG PICTURE;
A belief foisted on us,
Individuals, families, schools and restaurants
Are responsible for getting things under control,
Putting Germ Genies back in the bottle, the box.

Life at the bottom cannot escape
The belief a germ rules the world.
It holds humanity hostage,
In isolation,
At home,
With surefire delivery of the goods.
Let's stop making things easy for global leaders,
Those at center line, informing us all.

Stop owning responsibility,
Believing we do.
Be real.

Come out of isolation,
Draw heads from the sand
Long enough to see the light:
THINGS ARE OUT OF HAND.
Despite proliferating propaganda to the contrary,
We cannot be charged with the spreading germ or it's
clean up.

We are not responsible
And cannot continue to believe
Answers are in
Sterile hands,
Masked faces,
And separate rooms.
Solutions are expert-based,
Out of our hands, heads, and homes.

Let's courageously come clean,
Roll up our sleeves and get to the depths,
The bottom of this new reality,
The sudden shadowy net cast over humanity.
Like mustard gas, something smells fishy,
I say we follow our noses,
Clean up what stinks, starting at center line,
And the profiteers informing us all.

I know this is heresy,
And I truly don't care.
I'm ready to spread wings wide,
Leave behind beliefs created at center,
Watch bottomed-out reality
Fade to specks and disappear,
As I rise beyond the tainted fog,
Fully alive once more.

IRISH HERMITAGE DREAM

An invisible menace threatens.
I might blame the economy,
I could say it's people's indifference,
But it's not.
It is fear of the unknown, for sure.
An unlikely unknown;
As if lately, we're overshadowed by ghosts,
Phantoms from some dank corner of the collective mind.

Where once the group psyche held a semblance of
Peace and grace,
Darkness chokes out the light.
Marching heavy-footed into consciousness,
Innocent women deemed 'spoils' are cast down and raped.
Suspicious-looking individuals tortured for confessions,
Fodder for fashionable 'humane cruelty'.
Young soldiers bludgeoned,
Mired in their own bloody sludge.

From a hermit's cell in Ireland,
The long-dead Saint Kevin warns,
"Knocking such pesky visions from awareness,
Hain't yet thinkable.
Same as fleas on a dog,
Can chase the devils away, for one moment
Only to have 'em reappear in the next—
'Tis nothin' to do,
Lest like me, ye become reclusive."

From New York Harbor,
Lady Liberty's voice booms in retort,
"Try this—
Torch with my blaze, those marauding specters."

Elbow bent, she takes aim,
Shooting rays of red, green, and gold.
The Lady hits her mark, shrugs, and sighs,
"Alas, now we're naught, but witless."

Except to become hermits or feign rash ignorance,
There is no regenerating forsaken peace and grace,
No coming home to some idyllic state.
In today's war, does not matter where the battlefield,
The death toll rings,
Broadcast through every plane of sensibility,
Making sure the piper is paid in full.
And 'tis little to do for this blight on conscience, but suffer.

Time to recognize:
Warring itself must be conquered,
Every battle rounded up and scrutinized,
Like suspicious individuals
Sent to chambers for questioning,
Modern combat viewed as true 'spoils'
Must be thrown from patriotic pedestals,
Liberating minds bound exhaustively, in wars' bloody sludge.

Meanwhile, an invisible menace threatens.
I might blame the economy,
I could say it's people's indifference,
But it's not.
It is fear of the unknown, for sure.
But an unlikely unknown;
Overshadowed by ghosts,
Phantoms from our collective mind.

THE SWALLOWS OF CAPPUCCINO

"A non-fat,
No whip,
Mocha, please."
Minutes pass.
"Order
For Ike."
Got it. "Thanks!"

I tease students
About the choices
We make,
Impacting our lives
Much later.
Post mortem.
Our lives in the light.

After death,
We'll know
Full well
The influence of
Choices made
below, before.
Things chosen.

Something,
Anything,
Selected
Once or twice
A week,
Sticks to a soul
Like Velcro.

Forming
Bits of solid,
Standing light

That clogs
The flow of
Fluid radiance
In and around us.

"Another non-fat,"
Day after day.
Day in. Day out.
"No whip, mocha, please."
Minute's pass.
"Order for Ike."
Got it. "Thanks!"

Addictions,
Obsessions,
Stuff we ripen
Passion for,
Need every day,
More than once
Or twice.

Those solidify,
Layer, on layer.
Bank densely
Around us,
Until our own
Light dims.
In comparison.

And then, who gets attracted to us,
After death?
Souls with similar
Addictions, obsessions,
Passions.
With grand, solid
Mounds made of similar choices.

Non. Fat.
No. Whip.
Mocha.
For Ike—
Got it?
Yeah.
It's got you, too.

I tease my students,
Tell them to look for me,
On the other side.
They're apt to see
My tall, wide mountain of passion,
Emblazoned green and white,
With the Starbuck's coffee nymph.

Where I go next,
There will be
No Starbucks,
Not a coffee bar
Anywhere. Still,
Despite best intentions,
I'll look for one.

And attract, like swallows
To Capistrano,
Others
Impossible to see,
Due to the tall,
Wide masses of fixation
In the way.

The mountains will stand,
Until daily obsessions,
Addictions, passions
Wain from memory.

Is this heaven, hell,
Or the purgatory
In between?

"Non-fat,
No whip,
Mocha,
Please,
For Ike."
Got it.
No more.

Antone Grosz's *Letters to a Dying Friend* condenses after-death
experiences described at length centuries earlier in *The Tibetan
Book of the Dead*. I'm grateful for the abridged version. A portion
of it fell into place as the premise to this poem.

DOWN TO THIS

Telling the future,
We can.
I do, not always,
But in ways that count.
Divining truth
While others
Accept surface,
Whatever floats
To the top
Of everyday.
Not me, not always.
Hardly ever.

Preferring no glass
Half empty, half full,
Favoring no glass at all.
Getting to the bottom of things,
Every day—
Any day, or hour.
Crash through barriers,
Push past shallow,
Superficial.
Get underneath,
And overhead,
Into the mystical.

Telling the future,
Divining truth
About times to come,
Often looking
Back in time, then ahead.
Waves thrust forward,
Pass through generations.
I see the future eclipsed for me.

In my mother's generation,
Sixteen of eighteen cousins
End life's final decades with dementia,
Limping along midst debilitating cerebral scum.

Should the disease
Come my way,
As genetics lays bare
It's apt to do,
Swiping memories chronicled
While still mindful,
This collection of poems
Arrives quickly,
Full blown,
As if celestially sent,
For reading aloud to me later,
Much later by children and grandchildren.

Admittedly, the idea's stolen.
From Mike Nichols' *The Notebook*,
And from Laurie Hales Anderson, author of *Shout*,
Who recapped the highs—and lows—
Of her life in poetry,
Minus rhythmic staves.
Both inspired my writing,
And kept pages purring,
Whenever my idea engine
Seemed to sputter and choke.
Most dear to me,
Are these wise balladeers.

I am also grateful to the spirits
In charge of gifting the five senses
And the favor of memory.
I appreciate the cerebral accounts,
Particularly the very ones that find their way
From heart to mind, touching me today.

Should my life narrative go,
And the senses rip away,
I look forward to a new time and space,
Where sights, sounds, smells, and tastes reawaken.
I cannot imagine any heaven exists
Without such blissful promise.

ACKNOWLEDGEMENTS

This collection
written in Greece
while under the influence
of 2020 pandemic mayhem,
leaves me ever indebted
To Kalivia villagers
And Athenians too.
Their welcome
Care and concern,
Meeting a foreigner's needs
With kindness and diligence,
Day to day
Week after week
For months.
I thank you all.

I'm much obliged to readers,
including those plowing through
the choppy waves of early drafts:
Vanessa Dromen, Sophie Eagle,
Rochelle Carlson, Tane West and Betty Williams.

I am also grateful to the professionals at Atmosphere Press,
Drs. Kyle McCord and Trista Edwards, Alex Kale;
Designer Ronaldo Alves and his team,
Especially cover artist, Beste Miray;
Digital Director, Evan Courtright,
Publicity Director, Cameron Finch,
Production Manager, Erin Larson,
And any I missed,
Who place their fingers on the keys
Of book-crafting success at Atmosphere.

In the dance of acknowledgements
last, but far from least,
I must consider
the complex steps taken
by a global web
of family and friends,
students and associates—
time after time,
over countless years,
weaving the vivid colors
of constancy and devotion
into my cherished life.
I appreciate each of you.
From my heart.
Thank you all.

ABOUT ATMOSPHERE PRESS

Atmosphere Press is an independent, full-service publisher for excellent books in all genres and for all audiences. Learn more about what we do at atmospherepress.com.

We encourage you to check out some of Atmosphere's latest releases, which are available at Amazon.com and via order from your local bookstore:

I Rode the Second Wave: A Feminist Memoir, poetry by Fran Abrams

Dare To Love, poetry by RaLuca D. Gruin

Grief and Her Three Sisters, poetry by Jerry Lovelady

I Made A Place For You, poetry by Damian White

Melody in Exile, poetry by S.T. Brant

No better place than here, poetry by Dean Schabner

antidote to her ruin, poetry by prw

Loved By Fire, poetry by Natalie Rose

Covenant, poetry by Kate Carter

Near Scattered Praise Lies Our Substantial Endeavor, poetry by Ron Penoyer

Death Throes of the Broken Clockwork Universe, poetry by Wayne David Hubbard

Weightless, Woven Words, poetry by Umar Siddiqui

Journeying: Flying, Family, Foraging, poetry by Nicholas Ranson

ABOUT THE AUTHOR

Ike West in 1961

Ike West in 2021

An advocate for environmentally-safe prose of all shapes and sizes, Eileen 'ike' West, MA, is an international teacher and free-range writer featured in Susan Smit's *Wise Women* (NL 2003) and Susan Taylor's *Sexual Radiance* (US 1998). Across decades, West's essays liberally sprinkle magazines and other publications in the US, UK, Belgium, Austria, Italy, Greece, and the Netherlands. A sampling is available at ikewest.com. West's first poetry collection, *Whistler of Petty Crimes,* and earlier novels, *Away from Hannah's Castle* (US/NL 2006) and *Another Giant World* (UK 2018) are available through various and sundry book purveyors, including Amazon. Currently she keeps busy harvesting more oh-so poetic stories, and cobbling together her next volume, mostly about midlife misdemeanors.

For now, West's favorite petty crime: whistling out of tune.